SMALL TOWN KID

FRANK PREM

Published 2018 by Wild Arancini Press

Copyright © 2018 Frank Prem

All rights reserved. No part of this publication may be reproduced, stored in a retrieval system, or transmitted in any form or by any means, electronic, mechanical, photocopying, recording or otherwise, without prior written permission from the publisher.

A catalogue record for this book is available from the National Library of Australia.

Disclaimer

Some names, places and identifying details have been changed to protect for privacy and maintain their anonymity. I may have changed some identifying characteristics and details such as physical properties, occupations and places of residence.

This book contains cultural and indigenous references and language, for telling the story and is not meant to offend, or have any ill intent towards real life culture or indigenous people.

Every effort has been made to ensure that this book is free from error or omissions. However, the author, publisher, editor or their agents or representatives shall not accept responsibility for any loss or inconvenience caused to a person or organisation relying on this information.

Book cover design and formatting services by BookCoverCafe.com

First edition 2018

ISBN 978-0-9751442-3-7 (pbk)

ISBN 978-0-9751442-4-4 (e-bk)

This one is for Leanne,
who helps turn dreams into realities.

I can hardly wait to show you

july is finally gone and I am breathing
in the air of august
a taste of weather
that teases promise of days
when the sun is warm again
and the shivers worn since may
can be packed away for another season

I can hardly wait to take you
to the places where my spirit lies
along singing waters and scrubby creeks
the green and granite-bouldered hills
that never stop calling
and won't let me deny them

I want to show you where I grew
and what I saw when I was small
if something still remains of those things
so clearly drawn as pictures in my mind
of a small boy and his curious dog
with a long way to travel from breakfast
to the distant darkness of evening
on so many shining days

will you walk with me on a balmy afternoon
in the mayday hills and the woolshed valley
along the silver creek and past apple orchards
to the places where rabbits went to ground
at the sound of approaching adventurers
crossing old scars left by miners seeking gold dust
where I also found small treasures once

take my hand in the main street
of this town hewn from honey granite
I will tell you what once stood here and there
and you might help me rediscover what I knew
when I was in the springtime of my life
before an autumn season comes
to settle on my shoulders

I can hardly wait to show you

Contents

I can hardly wait to show you iv
oma rocks the cradle 1
working for a generation 2
poppy cakes 4
frenki boy 5
the exuberance of my aunt 7
you know mum's cooking 10
loss of faith 11
picnic story 13
from inside the outhouse 17
nightman 19
half moon at the trapdoor 21
the dawn of civilisation 22
butcher's paper 24
rabbit-o 26
the hallways of st joseph's 27
pine-needle tea and stabbing trees 28
spe-lli-ng b-y nu-mbe-rs 30
fast-track perambulation 31
pumpkin-rock terrorists 33
despatching tiny rubbish (and things like that) 35
facade catches 37
sunsets are 39
discovering tv 40
finch street elms 41
fires of autumn 43
at easter 44
a tricky place (the annual fete) 46
crackers 50

state of the art	56
relentlessness	58
holes in pockets	60
yonnie power	61
fight	63
hating whitey	66
mcalpine's cherries	67
sweet maureen	69
in the rooms	70
football and law	72
growing pains	73
swimming on the royal reserve	74
distance across ford street	75
on a new year's eve	76
libby's puzzle	77
finishing school and wedding maths	79
#1 finishing school	79
#2 wedding maths	80
not the *mandalay*	81
memorial park	82
a cocky's morning	84
between sink and stove	85
from the sticks	87
role to play	88
vale	89
palmer's not	91
small-town kids	92
broken english	93
circular square town	94
Other Works	95

Small Town Kid

oma rocks the cradle

while mama works
oma rocks the cradle
lulling the child
into slumber

the rhythm
soothes and settles

peace in the house

the afternoon passes
calm

~

in the early hours
fretful waking

dragging darkness

broken sleep

a weary journeying
to work
in the thinness
of morning

why will the child
not sleep
every blessed night
what is wrong with him

~

while mama works
oma
rocks the cradle

working for a generation

a small boy is at play

an older man
sits close by
on a chair
in contemplation
of what has been done
what progress made

considering the challenge
for tomorrow

a tree has been felled
and a photograph taken
to prove the victory

when the clean-up
is done
a garden will be dug
fruit trees planted

the man and his grown son
have laboured
and the days to come
will be the same
but
when finished
this work will stand
through generations

the boy is crying
calling to be picked up
and held

Small Town Kid

an encouraging word
and the lad rises
wandering closer
still sobbing
lying down again
this time at the old man's feet

his *opa* picks him up
and holds him
sitting in the chair
at the end
of the day
until the tears have stopped

poppy cakes

flowers of scarlet
grew in the garden

after the bloom
she would take the pod
into the mystery of her kitchen
to perform ritual magic

the cakes of my grandmother
were moist with overflowing flavour
deep crust filled with rich dark seed

an exquisite pleasure
and a small boy's
special and favourite treat

but that was before the law
brought a message
about the revised rules
of baking

no scarlet flowers grow
in the garden now
and I eat very little cake

frenki boy

mama called me
frenki boy
when I was a child
sometimes she said it
frenki yoy!
to make a point
about trouble I'd be in
if I didn't stop
what I was doing

yoy meni yoy frenki!!
I used to get a lot of that
though
for the life of me
I couldn't tell what *yoy*
I might have committed

it was a legacy
maybe
left to a small boy
from this other troubled guy
I used to hear about a bit

he was called
isus boga!
or something like that
and the women would make
a sign of the cross
with their hands
when they said it

but
in the evening
sometimes
mama would kiss me
and I'd become just
frenki moy

times like that
the day would end
okay

the exuberance of my aunt

my father's sister is getting older
though it took a long time to happen
I can see it in her face now
signs of age and recent strain

all through my small days
she seemed young and full of life
with exuberance held on a leash
lest it escape and betray a lack
of due decorum before the family
or even worse
in front of perfect strangers

looking back now I have a sense
that all the women in the family
moved through life with restraint

perhaps it was a cultural thing

I think small children can see
right through grown-ups
there's an instinct that operates
to let them know
when someone is hiding laughter
or when there is a genuine bite
awaiting the unwary
and I always felt that my aunt
was less dour than she implied

I can remember
when she married
in the town's fire station

it looks a very small place now
but with the two engines parked outside
and the station decorated into a hall
with tables and white cloths and balloons
crowded with people making merry
on convenient good spirits
and children chasing scatters of coins
thrown by guests honouring old custom
the station was a splendidness

and there was my aunt in her wedding-day glory
looking radiant
dancing a happy waltz
with every man
and with many of the women
and all of the children
each new partner pinning paper money
to her gown
as payment for the privilege

the folk music started
all bouncing piano accordions
and the rapid nimbleness of flying mandolins
rich voices and full harmonies

the dancing changed from waltz
to the darting feet
and swaying circles of the *kolo*
filling the hall with sound and movement
the crowd roaring songs
from both floor and table top
my aunt leading the joyous
overloud and rapid-fire chorus
of high-pitched squealing
that the women could do so well

Small Town Kid

ay-yay-yay-yay
ay-yay-yay-yay
yoh! yoh! yoh! yoh!

I've never forgotten my aunt
dancing and singing that night
the happy young bride laughing
with her exuberance for once
unrestrained
as I was falling asleep
in the corner of the fire station

you know mum's cooking

you know how sometimes your mum
can be really over the top
with cooking traditional food in the way
that she learned to do it back home
and most of the time it's sort of okay
or you don't really notice because
it's just there all the time
and sometimes it's really good
and you can feel clever about it
because the other kids' mums
don't know how to cook that good stuff
but sometimes it's that rotten spicy mince
wrapped up in cabbage leaves or
stuffed into capsicum and drowned
in some kind of red stewy sauce

you know *sarma* and *sattarash*

well I hate 'em

loss of faith

it is the women of my family
who are the keepers of faith
every sunday
and sometimes in the week
either early or late
in dresses that are restrained but fine
and with shawls rather than hats
to cover the head

our women wear no hats
but they pray
for the men and for the children
the passing over of our sins
and for those they left behind
in search of a better life
for their young

it is the women
who round up the men and the boys
to ensure attendance
at the small cathedral in the town
on the important days
for ritual expressions of faith

but when the letter for my mother came
in black-lined airmail
from the village of her parents
she wept with the bitterness
of injustice and loss and grief
she cried for so long
I was afraid
she would never stop

Frank Prem

god lost a believer
and I no longer needed
to make an appearance
at the sunday mass

Small Town Kid

picnic story

papa said
mama come on
we've got to get away
come on I want to
get away

mama pack
the picnic set
let's all
get away
mama I'm taking you away

hurry little children
we're almost
at the getaway
come on little children
today we'll get away

~

around the base of mount buffalo
between myrtleford and porepunkah
on the low green flats of king river
snuggled under the purple
of the uncleared slopes of the mountain
the business was mostly tobacco
from seedlings in hop gardens
to planting growing picking
and finally airing in rows of kilns
before packing leaf to market

a picnic visit to friends there
needed a whole weekend and three families
starting before one dawn and ending
not long before the next

the slaughtered pig was transported by the men
to an old bathtub for cleaning
in scalding hot water that made the flesh stink
and seared the skin for close shaving
with a deftly wielded cutthroat razor
honed for the job on an old leather strop
that reminded me overmuch of school

offal for sausages and exotic concoctions
was cooked in a squat laundry copper
heated by a small fire tended with loving care
to the right temperature by my father
who would often tell me
sonny
the only thing we waste from a pig
is the squeal

skewered on a wooden spit
the porker was stitched
with a belly full of apples and onions
before suspension above glowing coals
to slow roast

the women were responsible for cooking
for preparing sausages
and keeping up the food supply
the men were responsible for the pig

Small Town Kid

and for closely supervising the women
while consuming the pungent treasure
of liquid-fire *rakiya*
yielded by specially grown
and lushly productive white plums
intended for a higher purpose
than simply being eaten

it was the particular job of my *opa*
while he was sober enough
to sit at one end in the warm of the fire
and to turn the pig for hours over the coals
at just the right speed with the apples and onions
tumbling hollowly in a settled rhythm

sometimes when it rained
the job was only made tolerable
by the constant replenishment
of his rakiya supplies
to maintain internal warmth

on those occasions another man
would take over much earlier from opa
as was only right on a wet day

my own special job
was to keep well out of the way
by going with a friend into the low hills
with shotgun and rifle in hand
to frighten rabbits and snakes
until early evening brought us back
with the enticement of fresh-roasted pork
beckoning on the breeze

then singing dancing and mysterious card games
were played under lights that banished shadows
from the row of tobacco kilns
until the women put the children to bed
and the men could no longer stand

~

papa said
*mama come on
I want to dance with you
hey mama come and dance
it's good to get away*

from inside the outhouse

the door is basic timber
a z-frame
facing the inside
and a gap
at both top and bottom

the circulation of air
is important
in such a place

the room is small
weatherboard lined
with a tin roof
a one-seater
particularly suitable
as long-term residence
for both
spiders and flies

the hole of the seat is large
shiny smooth at the edges
from friction of skin
over the course of years

wide enough
and slippery enough
to swallow a small boy
whole
unless he is carefully perched
on the front edge
as he drums his feet
against the box

on the wall
is an area
kept clear of cobwebs
by the frequent movement
of purposeful hands

newspaper squares
are skewered on a wire hook
for the perusal
of partial stories and advertisements
from the popular press
before consignment
to a more noble cause

the creeper screen in front
is strategically grown
for concealment
from the main building
its pungent blooms a potent foil
for certain unmentionable aspects

it serves too
as the nest site
for a pair of blackbirds
that seem able to overlook
the patent fact
that this is
a low-rent neighbourhood

nightman

antiseptic tablets
poo
and pee

I suppose
that must be
what the smell is

always accompanied
by the incessant buzz
of fat blowflies
and the wriggling disgust
of yellow-white maggots

hallmarks
of the outhouse
at the back of the garden
as far from the residence
as possible

once each week
the nightman
in his dirty overalls
and smells
stops the truck
lined one side with full cans
the other with empties
outside on the street
in the early hours of morning
or after darkness
has fallen

always running
with an empty can
on his shoulder
up the length of the driveway
to the back
of the garden

a thump
on the outhouse wall
is his warning

open the trapdoor
full one out
swap the lids
new one in
thump the wall
all clear

hoist the full can
onto the shoulder
run
to the truck

he tripped once
and fell
all our recent history
exposed and putrid
on the road
in front of the house
where usually
we preferred to keep it
rather more
discreet

half moon at the trapdoor

twin pink half-moon
expanses of flesh protrude
almost disembodied
from a snug fit
that seals the wooden circle
tightly

two small watchers
suppress a giggle
overawed at the sight
stolen through the gap
at the top
of the trapdoor

the dawn of civilisation

a whistle shrieks
in mid-morning
just before
the thunder of a blast
from down in the gorge valley

the sound marks
rock-smashing progress
in the forward creep
of the sewerage line

it's a signal
of the end of days
for the outhouse
and the nightcart
arriving in the form
of filtration
and treatment plant
and of sculpted porcelain
for the forging
of a modern town

but the excitement comes
at evening
in the exploration
of new rock formations
and the exposed white heart
of a granite boulder

it lies in the marvel
of smooth semicircles
in broken rock
drill holes
that held explosive charges

Small Town Kid

it is in the finding and collection
of the red- yellow- blue- and green-
coated copper wire
that conducted the impulse
and triggered the bang

it is in these small proofs
of being there
at the dawn of civilisation

butcher's paper

thursday

gather the papers
and lay them out flat
then carefully make
a tight roll

tie the bundle
with a length of string
and a butterfly knot
hoist the load
onto a shoulder
and start walking
up to ford street
and spencer's butcher shop

the butcher-man
in his stained blue-stripe apron
smiles
and cracks a little-kid joke
in the cool shopfront
that smells the particular smell
of fresh meat and sawdust

he puts the bundle
on the scales
to measure by weight
the value
of the popular press
in recent times

Small Town Kid

sixpence
for a couple of pounds of paper
and the news
becomes the wrapping
for another feed
of tender young chops

rabbit-o

a line of nails
head high on the paling fence
a sharp knife
and fast hands
are the basic requirements
of the rabbit-o

a hundred pair of bunnies
after a night of spotlighting
or setting traps
need speed
in the emerging sun of morning

gutted and skun
in thirty seconds each
skins are stretched wide to dry
inside out on wire
red meat is placed on white ice
fast
to avoid the risk of spoiling
before delivery to customers
as the day heats up

~

would you like a pair missus
they're fresh this morning
your husband did some work for me
and I want to say
ta

Small Town Kid

the hallways of st joseph's

in the hallway at st joseph's
whooshing cane makes contact
with a naked calf

the sound lingers
inside memory
longer than the holding back
of smarting pain
gulping tears
and brave facades

longer than the raw red marks
etched in an early mind

good morning mother superior
will you correct the sins I've committed
I'm not sure what they are
but I guess you're here to show me

I'm here to be educated

pine-needle tea and stabbing trees

the girls are sweeping

they've built a playhouse
under the trees
at the back of
the old *hossie*
derelict hospital grounds
that adjoin the primary school

each lunchtime
they sweep the rooms they've created
by laying out red bricks
in a large square

they visit one another

would you care for
dirt- and pine-needle tea

ahhh
simply delicious

and tell me
how is your dolly going

the boys are busy too

six of them
have found sturdy twigs
with the right shape
and a good grip

they are spitting onto bricks
and rubbing the sticks
backward and forward

Small Town Kid

sharpening the ends
to form wicked points
waving their arms
through the air
in a practice motion

when they're ready
a line forms

the first boy sets off at a run
straight at the soft bark
of a hundred-year-old
redwood

he doesn't stop
but climbs it
using momentum to go higher
than yesterday

at the apex
he stabs the twig
into the tree
leaving it in place
as he comes to ground

there

the new mark
has been set

Frank Prem

spe-lli-ng b-y nu-mbe-rs

I learned to spell in small numbers
multiples of three
has five and one remainder
mul-tip-les-oft-hre-e

sometimes
I would mis-spell words deliberately
to keep the numbers neat
I do not like remainders-s

that was seven   (four)

I gu-ess- it's- ski-rti-ng o-n ob- ses-sio-n
bu-t I d-on't- thi-nk t-hat- mat-ter-s to-o mu-ch

when I was small people used to think
that I was saying the words under my breath
moving my lips as children do when reading
but I was counting in threes
to the end of the word   the line   the page

spelling in small numbers

I so-met-ime-s do- it s-til-l

fast-track perambulation

the driveway is only
two ragged lines
of uneven red brickwork
sloping down to the footpath
and the street

the old pram is a conveyance
for wailing small folk
used once upon a time
a while ago

the wheels go around
in locomotion
when propellant of the right kind
is applied

the race team
are motoring enthusiasts
with a need to feel the wind
rushing through their hair

take your seat
hold on
keep your head low

with one big push
the track
is all downhill

whip past the border shrubs
through the gates
over the gutter bridge
sail
or fly
across the road

no time for steering
brakes are for babies

drag it back
do it again

next champion
assume your position
please

pumpkin-rock terrorists

pumpkin rock is a massive boulder
towering precariously above the tourist road
that encircles the scenic gorge
and wanders through spectacular
granite ranges
allowing visitors to marvel
at views of the most historic gold town
in northeast victoria

visitors should set out from the notable
golden horseshoe monument

pause
for a moment
at the glorious
old gunpowder magazine

take the opportunity
to walk around
the replica slab hut

then drive a little further
to enjoy the vista
of beautiful woolshed creek valley
proceed past pumpkin rock
and on
until the road ends
above the old tannery
at newtown falls

make the trip
by car or by bus
in less than an hour

enjoy the sights

we apologise
for the unscheduled stop
to clear the road
of suspiciously aligned branches
and medium-sized rocks
too large to be driven over
or around

apologies also
for the sound of laughter
drifting from the top
of pumpkin rock
where two small tourist terrorists
maintain their surveillance
while sharing sandwiches from home
and striking a blow
in revolt against the invasion
of rubbernecks
and sticky noses

Small Town Kid

despatching tiny rubbish (and things like that)

it was only
meant to be
a tiny fire
to rid us of
small rubbish
and things like that

but the wet
and the wind
made burning tough
and an accelerant
is supposed
to do things
faster

how was I to know
there could be danger
from conflagration
leaping up
a petrol spout

and how was I to know
that green grass
could burn
as fast as dry
or that flame
would have a life
all of its own

Frank Prem

I was only
fire-dispatching
tiny rubbish

being helpful

and things like that

Small Town Kid

facade catches

a clean sound

thock

and the ball is on the way back

time it right

wait

then
dive-clutch-roll-rise
with the ball in hand

hold it up
to the adoring crowd

another batsman
dismissed
in this crucial game
of myth test cricket

then up the ball goes
again

thock

~

the facade is all that's left
of the first hospital
built in the town
way back in eighteen-something

high up
look closely
inside the granite triangles

Frank Prem

the signature markings
of a young boy's dream
live in the shapes
left behind by a muddy tennis ball
on a solitary day
after rain

sunsets are…

for packing up the wickets
and calling stumps to end the session

for answering the call
to come inside for dinner

for feeding the dog and making sure
he is patted well

for taking shoes off at the door
so no dirt or mud comes inside

for watching the kookaburra
silhouetted against the red sky

in a branch of the dead gum tree
laughing at the end of day

discovering tv

if you walk
along the streets
in the heat
of the summer evening
you may note the blue glow
and irregular pulsing of light
that illuminates each house

muted voices
come from patios
and lounge rooms
to compete with the crickets
and cicadas
of a warm night

lights are off
and whole families have moved
out onto verandas
bringing chairs
and three-bum vinyl sofas
or sitting on the concrete

whiling away
flickering dark hours
and mesmerised
in the sensation
of discovering tv

finch street elms

the elm trees
lining finch street
must have stood
for eighty or ninety years

they are a grand parade
despite the annual autumn butchery
to ensure safety for
or perhaps from
the power lines
that thread and join them
like knots placed at regular intervals
on a length of string

these elms are a marker
for the passage of seasons

the fall of hops
precedes the opening
of deep-green summer leaves
and forms a soft
crinkling carpet
to cover the holes
of seven-year cicadas
whose cast-off shells
are scattered skeletally around the base
of late spring

red and yellow weeks
lead to trails of rising smoke
from house-proud frontages
that burn cleansing fires
throughout autumn

Frank Prem

and hint
at the grey days to come
when the leaves
have all fallen
and bare black branches
stand deserted
and stark
in the frost-brittle cold
and stillness
of winter

fires of autumn

on the nature strip
in front of each house
leaves are raked into small heaps
below the exposed branches
of a long street lined with naked elms

the crumpled sheets of yesterday's news
are inserted
to the centre of each
yellow gold and brown pile

cold stillness awaits
the striking of a match
and the rising taste of smoulder

the time has come
let the fires of autumn
be lit

at easter

they've started early this year
it's not yet half past six
but the main roads are barricaded and attended
to divert traffic

golden balloons are being inflated
to form two vibrant arches
one each side of the main intersection
where the parade will pass
in a homage to the local legend
of a horse shod in golden shoes
back in the days of the rush
when this small town and its rich fields
were a glittering power

the vintage bakery van
is in the street
it's about a thousand years old
and restored in shining red

last year they offset the wheels
to make it bobble up and down in the parade
on pencil-thin tyres
like a clown car

trestles and marquees are being erected
food and music
trinkets craft and produce
all will be on display
before the main event
around noon

~

Small Town Kid

and here we are
the family gathered at easter
from melbourne and adelaide
by train and by car
to fill my parents' house
with talk and consumption
reminiscence and warmth

we too are celebrating
not easter
but ourselves
the fact of us through the years
and our own legends

later we will witness the parade
visit the family outliers
bask in the pleasure
of this occasional rejuvenation

we will remember ourselves
as we were
and reflect on the paths we have travelled
before returning to witness again
the easter parade

a tricky place (the annual fete)

the c-of-e churchyard
with its granite tower and solid isolation
is a tricky place

draped in solemn appearance
and with an air of long abandonment
held lazily in the overgrown waving
of dry grass
dilapidated outbuildings
leaning posts and loose wire netting
hardly hint at a time before neglect

it seems small now
almost shrivelled
lifeless

~

once a year
it happens once a year
the noise shatters the afternoon
as an old ute with two loudspeakers
attached above the roof of the cabin
does circuits of the town
and can be heard in a garbled blur
from three streets off
and not much better up close

Small Town Kid

but it doesn't matter what they're saying
because we already know

the preparations have been happening
for days
and we've watched as the main arena
has been swept clean
the fences mended
and mountings for the short logs
beaten into firm position
for the woodchoppers to go at it

the mugs are to start at nine or ten
and the call winds down
backwards
to zero
before the scratch marker swings his axe

the o'toole boys are unbeatable
and will put the blade
through a short log from left to right
first on one side and then the other
leaping off the mountings a single stroke
before those with a nine-second start

we know that the clowns
will be moving their heads
slowly from side to side
tempting us to put a ping-pong ball
inside their gaping mouths
and that the bamboo hoops might be rewarding
if one would only fall properly
around the prize

and that knocking down blocks with a ball
is easy
until you have just two left standing
while pinging ducks with a slug gun
would be a piece of cake
if they would stop moving so fast

we tasted the fairy floss last year
and pronounced it good

there has already been talk
about sneaking away from mum and dad
to smoke a secret cigarette
and about which girl might be tempted
to try a first kiss or ...

there may be a sausage sizzle this year
if the grass isn't too dry
with the risk of fire

the merry-go-round is reserved
for little kids
and all of them will be there
with people from town
and from the local farms
chatting in groups
and walking in their good clothes
through the heat of the evening

to the spinning wheel where there are
four tickets left for a shilling
who wants these last four tickets
and any pick of the prizes on the third shelf

Small Town Kid

*we can't spin the wheel till we've sold
the last two tickets*

are you ready

spinning now

*it's number twenty-five blue
who's got twenty-five blue*

*come on up elsie and help yourself
to something from the third shelf*

~

this churchyard is a tricky place
in its abandonment

it looks like nothing has happened here
for a very long time

crackers

late october

the temperature is rising
as each day passes

in scattered paddocks
fallen branches
old and dry
are being gathered and heaped

car tyres
scrounged through the year
are strategically placed
at the bottom

in the centre

higher

paper boys are collecting
from the newspaper shop
where mr carter is the chief supplier
for the town

of *red devils*
in different shapes and sizes
in *tom thumb* strings
and wrapped packets
of *ha'penny*
penny
and giant *tuppenny* bangers

sky rockets and *roman candles*

Small Town Kid

shoe boxes fill
ahead of time
with occasional pistol cracks
here and there
to test the merchandise

excited discussions are being held
in the schoolyard
about plans and preparations

about the best ways
to extract one half of a doubled wick
to extend it beyond
its original capabilities

about how to twirl together two
or even three or four
similarly treated explosive devices
to create formidable weaponry

theorising about the optimal way
to seal a big banger
in a can
for underwater experimentation
and the creation of submerged booms
and rising spouts
of dirty yellow water

~

early november

the possible threat
of total fire ban
looms
as potential catastrophe

mountains of raised wood
in the paddocks
crowned with effigy
and scarecrow
rise all around the town
with still more fuel to be added
while the days last

everywhere
arsenals have been formed
gathered and stored

waiting

the fathers of those
without enough pocket money
to lay in a stash
are badgered without mercy almost to the point
of revealing a secret hoard
too early
in the face of such sweating anxiety

but the *jumping jacks* stay hidden
or are simply denied
until the time is right
and the day has come
at last

then
in the fading light
the bonfire
on the far side of the beechworth gorge
is touched off
to blaze red at the town
and signal that the time
is now

Small Town Kid

and suddenly
it's fire everywhere
and the people glow

dads are drinking beer
under pressure
to provide the traditional bottle launcher
for the rockets to fly into the air
and explode
the little kids stumbling backwards
in awe

while the tom thumbs rattle
and the rat-a-tat sound
establishes the tone
for cracker night

~

and I am off
with my swagbag on my shoulder
to visit half a dozen places
where the thick black stench of rubber
burning slow
is my guide

throwing ha'penny bangers
as close as I dare
to make a kid
concentrating hard on a short wick
jump high
almost out of his skin

and chasing after duds
that didn't explode
as they should

searching for a second chance
to relight
a remnant fuse
fanning it back to sputtering life

also a chance
to go deaf
as it explodes
right beside my ear

I can't hear a thing
except for the bells now ringing in my ears
but I'm still blasting away
on the far side of town
until the fires have died a little
and the crowd
is starting to go home

a couple of *tuppenny* bangers
and a short detour
to blow up the deputy headmaster's mailbox
is an annual event
and he's long practiced
at straightening its swollen metal sides
on the morning after

I've still got some ammunition left
but
better not let them off
right now
there's a message
in the silence of the dark
that cracker night
is almost done

Small Town Kid

tomorrow
we'll be scouring paddocks
for the duds and the squibs
to break in half
so the black powder shows
and then lighting them
to make an angry fizzer
for a moment
until they're gone

the tyres still burn
and glow
to show us where the action was
and the ringing in my ears
like cracker night
is passing
slowly
from my mind

state of the art

frank would rather ...

bloody mr mussen

who does he think he is

I don't reckon he's ever liked me
and he never
ever
gives me a fair go

... spend all his time ...

anyway
art is a crappy subject
and he's a lousy teacher

so what if I can't draw

papier-mâché is just messy rubbish

... flirting with the girls ...

and I don't

I

do

not

flirt with the girls

Small Town Kid

I only mess around a bit

he just can't teach

... than learning art ...

oh man

mum's going to eat me
for this report card

relentlessness

I think I sense
a little weakness
don't you

she looks
a bit nervous
wouldn't you say

she isn't very sure
of herself
that's obvious

what if we just
ignore her
when she speaks
and do some
clowning around
instead of working

I don't reckon
she can handle it
what do you think

let's do something
secret and silly
up the back

ha
she's started yelling
and she looks red
losing it

look
she's brought a newspaper
reading it

Small Town Kid

instructions on the board
not even trying
to talk to us

I think we've got her

is this the first time
it's happened
it must be

I've never seen
one cry
like that before

I wonder
what we can do
next

holes in pockets

cigarettes can burn holes
in a pocket
when a teacher
gets too close

and that
makes it hard to hide
a small habit
from the danger
of a mother's investigations

do you suppose
he was talking
just as a way
of passing time

maybe
rising smoke
was making him think
of fire

and I wonder if he knows
that by standing
for so long
too close
he was causing
danger
to our young
and tender lives

because
cigarettes
can burn holes

yonnie power

the street boy is out
again

sullen in the pull
and push
of adolescence
he has grown more comfortable
alone

in this town the boys learn early
the art of throwing stones

piffing a yonnie
at cans
at trees
road signs

skimming across the lake

discouraging a dog
from following

seeing how close you can get
to a kid who's across the road

one of the dreaded multitude
of atkinsons
who'll *piff* one at you
if you aren't quick enough
to get in first

tonight
it could be either
skill refinement
or energy conservation

Frank Prem

but one way
or another
the street light
on the church corner
is about to be
extinguished

fight

tension builds
from sunday

through a week
of minor huddles
that materialise
and dissipate
on street corners

and where the local lads
the ones with wheels
and those merely
in attendance
half form tactical groups
for a moment

to plot
make arrangements
for the coming friday

anticipation melds
with the planning
of ways to set the scene
for the great
get-even
with the smartarse fools
from the other town
who have no right
to claim ascendancy

self-respect screams
for vengeance

next friday

~

there are thirty
or more
around the two
at the side of the street
in the granite gutter

chosen site
for the confrontation

knuckles and knees
punctuated by
the soft dull thud
of a metal pipe
striking home

among raw grunts
and muffled kicking
the stranger is downed
according to plan

the esteem
of the town
undergoes a restoration
with each connecting strike

Small Town Kid

the sound of the blows
in the eerie near-silence
is a pulse beat that reaches
to touch the young witness
running for home
with his eyes fixed
wide open

hating whitey

I never knew
what hate really was
until bloody whitey cropperson
so-called men's barber
did a short-back-and-sides
on me

like a little boy
or an old man

he's nothing but
a bloody butcher
and I will never
go there
again

mcalpine's cherries

in the weeks of heat and holidays
the cherry-lined branches
are burdened deep purple
or black or red
with the promised succulence
revealed through the light loam dust
raised by a shower of passing rain

the trees stand
in leafy straight lines
over and around the hillside
categorised by variety
and the timing of their readiness
set wide enough apart
for the tractor to deposit and collect
bins of the picked fruit
taken singly or in joined clusters
of twins and triplets
that may straddle a teenage ear
in a moment of unproductive decoration

the gun pickers
fill their buckets in what seems
like just a moment
up and down the ladders
to strip a tree
and move to the next
in the time it takes
to have a good look around
and a sip of tea
from the thermos

my paltry efforts might be improved
if I wasn't afraid of ladders
since the apples of last season
flung me to the ground

and perhaps I'd last longer
before getting sacked
if my friend and I
weren't fighting
cherry-dodging battles with juicy missiles
flying between adjoining rows
to the irritation of the boss
old mac mcalpine
during his daily inspections
of the adequacy and progress
being made by the casual labour

his free advice to novice pickers
resounds with a wealth of acquired
orchardist wisdom and kindliness
when he tells us in a burred brogue

b-h-o-o-ys
if youre going to eat em
eat the bir-r-r-d pecked ones
theyr-r-e the sweetest

good advice
but after three days
I never wish to see or to touch
one of those red devils again

sweet maureen

I rode my bike
for sweet maureen
from beechworth to yackandandah

fourteen miles
of love-smit pedalling
down the hill
of the rising sun

a million miles an hour
not fast enough
but my breath
was taken away

I was drawn
down the road
descending like a bullet
from the barrel
of my rifle

drawn to ride
to sweet maureen

in the rooms

have you been in the rooms
before they come out to play
while they're all milling around
in half states of pulling on shorts
kicking the ball to each other
and clacking precariously on timber floors
in black boots with leather stops
tapped in tight by the studder
mr jackson
who looks after the mental-hospital garden
during the rest of the week

the boys are all shining from oil rubbed on
and the room reeks of the liniment they use
so I can hardly breathe
but I drag the air in deep
until I can feel menthol down to my toes
and I become a bit like these fellows
who are about to take the field on my behalf
and for a little town that manages to grow mighty
for two hours each winter saturday afternoon

two at a time
they lie full stretch on the bench
muscles gleam
loose and smooth
and moving
as though they have a life of their own
under the fast-sliding hands
of the white-overalled trainer
who taught woodwork
to my class at school just yesterday

Small Town Kid

come on you supporters
gather round in a circle just behind the players
a bit of shoosh please
the coach has got a few words to say
before the game starts

about doing it for the town
about doing it for the team
about doing it for each other

let's do it
carn the bombers!

football and law

woe to those
who meet the policeman
when the bomber boys
don't kick straight

dragged off the street
slapped in the face
and a foot up the arse
till you're falling

if it's saturday
we better all be praying
for the bombers to win
or it's a copper
at war with the world
again

sergeant mozza o'byrne
stalking the streets
looking for a victim

growing pains

a child of the nighttime
he walks
alone
with just the moon
to cast an eye
on his path

he wanders
through streets that lie empty
at the end of daylight

only his footfalls
echoing softly
break the silence he meets

and nobody knows
why he's out walking
or what's in his mind
where he goes

the night is private
the dark conceals

around the cloak
of a black mystery
soft hope lingers
that it's only growing pains
that one day
he will walk in the light

swimming on the royal reserve

stewie shouldn't go swimming
on hot evenings
with his belly full
of royal reserve port

it's cheap by the flagon
but
it doesn't aid
his buoyancy

there'll be a day
when we don't find him
floating
like we did last night

or when we don't start
to look
quite soon enough

if the silly bugger
goes and drowns himself
we'll all be in strife
with the law
and our parents

the whole damn town

distance across ford street

the dolphin cafe is the ideal spot
to watch the shadow
slipping across ford street

a journey wide enough
to last you
all your life

there's only pinball
and cigarettes
under-age
six-pack saturdays

hiding
from the watchers
riffling curtains
at every window

and there's cheating
with cunning stealth
the best efforts
of the law

it's slow breathing
slow walking
slow living
to last forever

or just until the shadow
makes the other side
of ford street

on a new year's eve

judy runs the supermarket now
but I remember her as fifteen years
of laughing dark-brown eyes
that once upon a time
closed to kiss me
on a new year's eve
in a crowded street
that vanished
for the whole
of one
single
moment

libby's puzzle

little libby was
the runt in a line
of older sisters
and bigger brothers

everything in the world
was already known
before she came along
and someone else
owned all the simple answers

she
was the only mystery left
in a tiny universe
a puzzle
growing up and searching
for her own pieces

some of the boys
tried to help her out
by touch
but they only
added clouds
to the picture

by the time
we visited the fairway
near the green
she was already tired
drifted beyond caring
my clumsy presence
more hope than help

for her it was already
just an old habit
but I at least
felt some pieces move
in a pursuit
of higher learning

finishing school and wedding maths

#1 finishing school

she was always popular
in the middle of things
pretty
and she was a flash
across a hundred yards
on sports days

she met a guy
who drove a loud machine

he used to pick her up
after school
or talk across the fence
at lunchtime
and during recess

he kissed her
till it made our eyes pop
with wonder
and whispers

he drove her
all the way
from high school
interstate
to maternity

she stopped coming
to classes
then moved away
before the baby arrived

#2 wedding maths

country folk
are highly skilled
at finessing mathematics
complex problems
reduced
to simple calculation

start by adding
the number of days
between dispatch of invitations
to blushing of bride

then multiply
the factors suggested
by a hint of swelling
caught in a glimpse
of profile
to raise the inherent probabilities
of every possible date
from conception to delivery

complete the sum
by tut-tutting
at a gown
that should not be
quite so white

not the *mandalay*

I thought the *mandalay*
for a first little taste
in a foursome
her guarantee
of safety

but no friends came along
the mandalay was dark
and closed
nowhere to go

what to do
feeling foolish

but we found a pub
with a band and a tune
for a shuffle over the floor
so much closer
than what I'd planned

an intoxication

words lost and found
words left unsaid
a song
raised for us

the first singing

memorial park

under the embrace
of warm night
the trees of memorial park
are majestic and imposing
in the darkness

ancient californian redwoods
bunya pines
and giant conifers
tower silently
as though waiting for us
to lie beneath them

on the soft grass
below the triumvirate
of children's swings
rotunda
and a monument
to those
who will never have
our chance

we can only gaze
upwards
between the disappearing
lines of trees
to the movement of clouds
above the silhouetted branches

Small Town Kid

breathless in excitement
awed by wonder
at words spoken
secrets revealed
and promises made
for tomorrow

a cocky's morning

christmas beetles
carrion
and paddocks bathed in heat

scrawny cows
with white in their eyes
awaiting milking
for relief

a big-striding man
walks across the yard
to survey
another day

seven mornings
in a week
the same damn things
just like it's always been

not a lot
to laugh about
not much
to raise a smile

the season is shot
and the politicians
are bad
add a useless new son-in-law
and the cocky's lot
is a pain
in the arse

always
a pain in the arse

between sink and stove

if we look in mcphail's
we might find what we want
they don't do much new
but it'll function all right

old wardrobes with drawers
two for our room
one for the spare
is that enough
will it do

we've got space for a dresser
if the money will last
but first
a crib and change table
for the nursery

hey I think we'll get by
won't our folks
be surprised
they think that we're lost
but I don't suppose
we're so bad

will you dance me
my dear
in this ballroom of ours
I can almost embrace you
when I reach
right around

yes dance with me
bride of mine

between sink
and stove
an orchestra's playing

from the sticks

there's chicken shit
on the boots of the boy
who came to the smoke
from northeast victoria

speaking too slow
and walking with a roll
grown on steep murmungee hills
above white foggy mornings
his eyes are as wide
as collins and elizabeth
streets that stretch
so much longer than a day
with the dog and the traps

he's some kind of a wonder
probably it's the weathered hat
or maybe the patchwork sheepskin coat
but he's surely now
a captive
and a wonder

role to play

sometimes in the night
the child is sleeping
sometimes
I watch over
my tiny wonder

hold my breath
lest a sound escape
think
what role
might I play

in the making
and in the shaping
of the future
dreaming there

and sometimes
it's in the late of night
I toss and turn
and I ponder

what good role
for that sleeping child
what's my role
to play

no answers
in the nighttime
maybe tomorrow

maybe some time

maybe answers
one other day

vale

driving the night
travelling home
from a gathering at some party
in myrtleford

oncoming lights sway
and weave
hypnotising in dance

slow down
pull over
stop the car
watch and wait them
to pass

~

five minutes from home

three minutes delay

ten minutes post contact

they are gone

~

mothers shed tears
while fathers just stare
and friends can't believe
these were the ones
that we loved

christine and jill
where are you
where are you
why won't you answer
when we call

palmer's not

for mick who didn't make it

palmer's not swinging on her arm tonight
he got delayed somewhere
she'll have to make do with the rest of us
take a drink and kill the hours

palmer's not eating what his mama cooked
he's not sleeping in his bed
we set a place but I might help myself
to an extra serve of egg and a sausage

palmer's not turning up on time at work
he must have overslept
the boss is talking about stopping his pay
and I think we're going to be on overtime

palmer's not collecting for the tipping pool
he didn't lay the bets last week
somebody else ought to take the job
because the horses are still running

palmer's not marrying next saturday
and he didn't pay for my tuxedo
the bride's putting back the wedding gown
but
I'll see you at the church

small-town kids

it seems long ago
we were just kids
watching time pass away

in a place where open space
formed the barriers and walls
of nowhere to go

growing without mirrors
our young eyes never noticed
the fleeting glimpses
of mental barricades

and day upon day
we were formed
as small-town kids

was there ever a chance

broken english

I can hear it on the streets
like when I walk into a milkbar
to get a paper in the morning

the guy will say something
to his lady or the kids

doesn't matter where he's from
I can mostly understand it

I hear it when a woman rings the phone
and I tell her she's got a wrong number
she says *sori*
she meant to dial somebody else
but the sound of her voice is so familiar
it makes me want to go back
to see the people that say

frenki
kako si
you go okay
frenki boy
good
good
dobro

I wonder how my *mutti* is
what *tata* has been getting up to
and *oma* and *teta*
uncle *damyan*

it's time to go home

circular square town

I'm watching a circle form

from the start
at the point where I had to leave

within the arc
that constantly drew me to return
never once letting go

to the place where I stood
away out
on the perimeter
of being an independent man

how many radial steps
did it take
to pace from youth
into middle years

to this moment
a return to the beginning

the old town is different now
so am I
but the circle
is set to be squared
at last

Other works

The Book of Evenings, 2003 (written as Frank Faust). Currently out of print.

Memoir of a Dog, 2008. Currently out of print.

CPSIA information can be obtained
at www.ICGtesting.com
Printed in the USA
LVHW081440090519
617253LV00032B/750/P